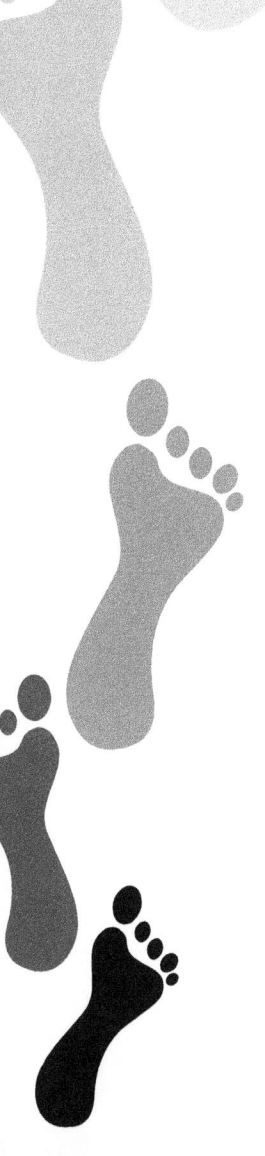

To Toni Philanda and Opal Lynnette:

May the creative talents that you are blessed

with leave foot prints for others to follow.

FOOTSTEPS TO FOLLOW

By
Opal R. Wilkerson

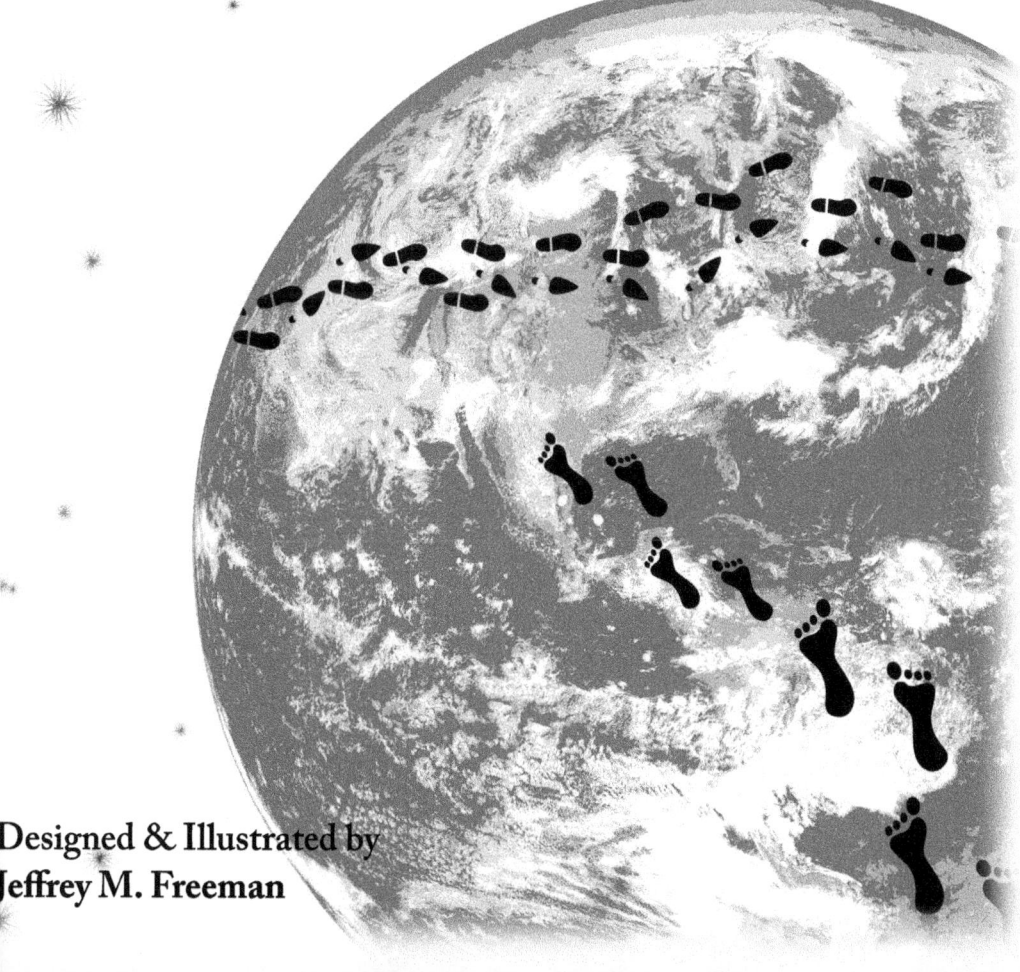

Designed & Illustrated by
Jeffrey M. Freeman

Published 2023, Ingram Spark

ISBN 979-8-218-25794-1

Author: Opal R. Wilkerson

This book illustrated and designed by:
Jeffrey M. Freeman • Email: jfreeman101@gmail.com

Opal R. Wilkerson was born in Brownsville, Tennessee to Opal Taylor Springfield and Tonnie Springfield in 1945. Opal attended Morristown Junior College in Morristown, Tennessee and D.C. Teachers' College in Washington, D.C. There she received her B.S. Degree in Elementary Education. She also did graduate studies at Bowie State University, Trinity College, and Georgetown University.

Opal taught elementary school in Washington, D.C. for thirty years. She also taught elementary school in Prince Georges' County Public School for nine years. Opal retired from Prince Georges' County Public School in June, 2011. Since her retirement, Opal has enjoyed taking classes with other seniors at Prince Georges' County Community College and writing. Opal has written several poems and one children's book. Her book was published in the spring of 2023. The title of her book is "The Prettiest Butterfly Contest." It is on sale at Barnes and Noble and Amazon Books.

Let's make known the many untold facts,

about our people we call Blacks.

It will sure be a source of inspiration,

Which will help others reach their destination.

From it we will develop that needed pride.

Truth about Black History, we must reveal and not hide.

So tell the story of each gifted black life,

How each won the victory over injustice

and strife.

Tell of their struggles to reach life's mountain top.

With determination and courage they did

not stop.

These were the characteristics of each famous

black scholar.

And each did leave footsteps for us to follow.

Medicine

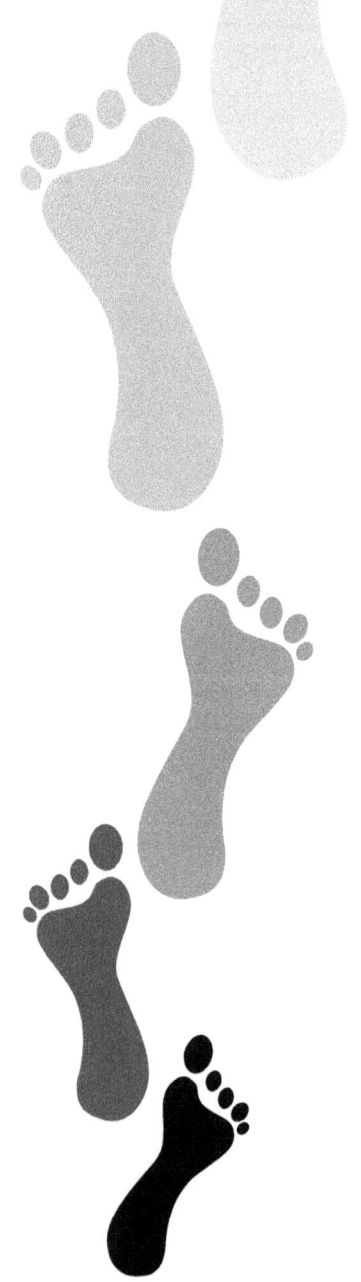

In medicine,

Charles Drew and

Daniel Hale Williams a

path did start,

From saving blood plasma

to surgery of

the opened heart.

Charles Drew

Daniel Hale Williams

Science

George Washington Carver
and Benjamin Banneker made
steps in the scientific field,
From designing the first clock to
discovering the many products that
peanuts can yield.

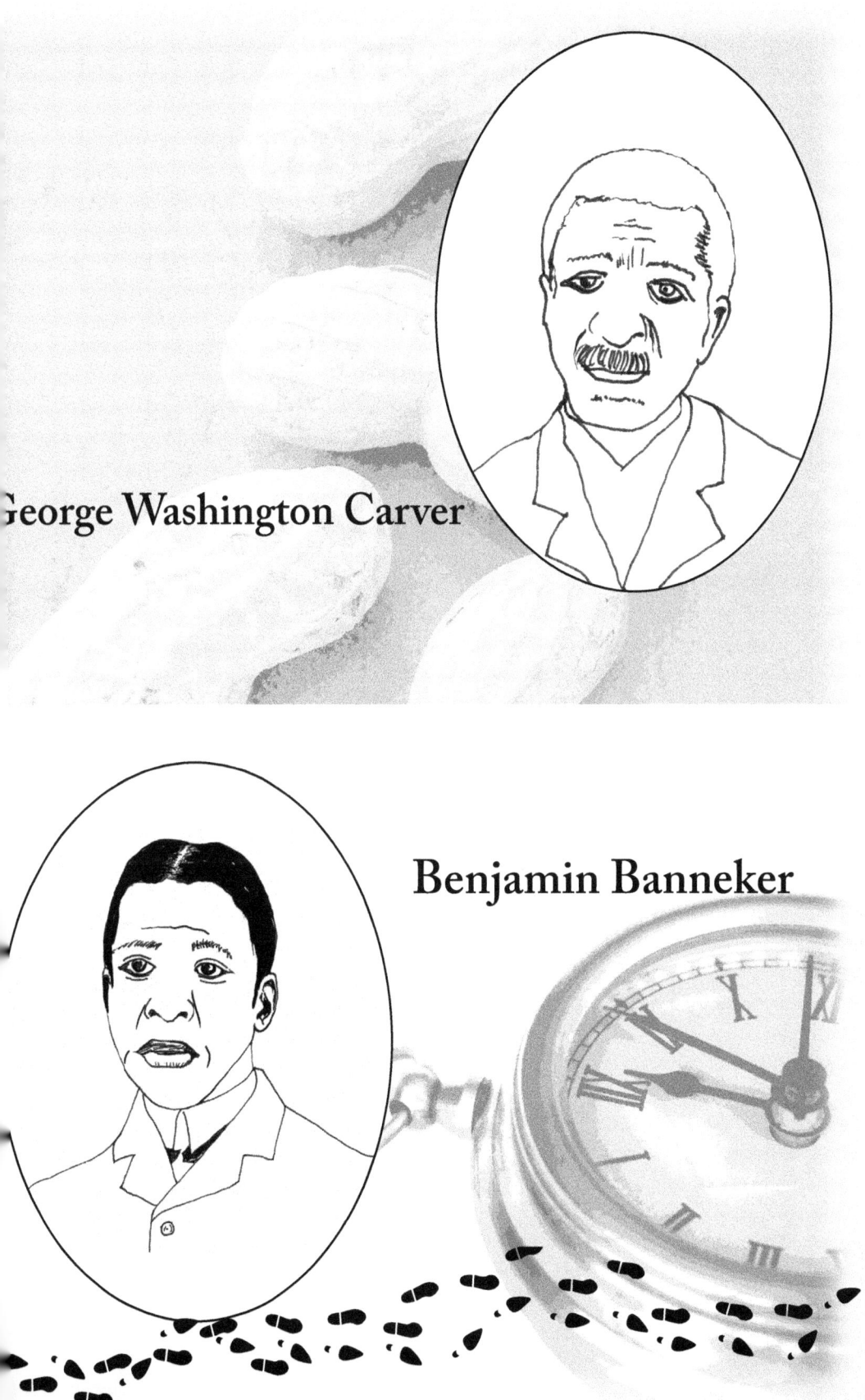

George Washington Carver

Benjamin Banneker

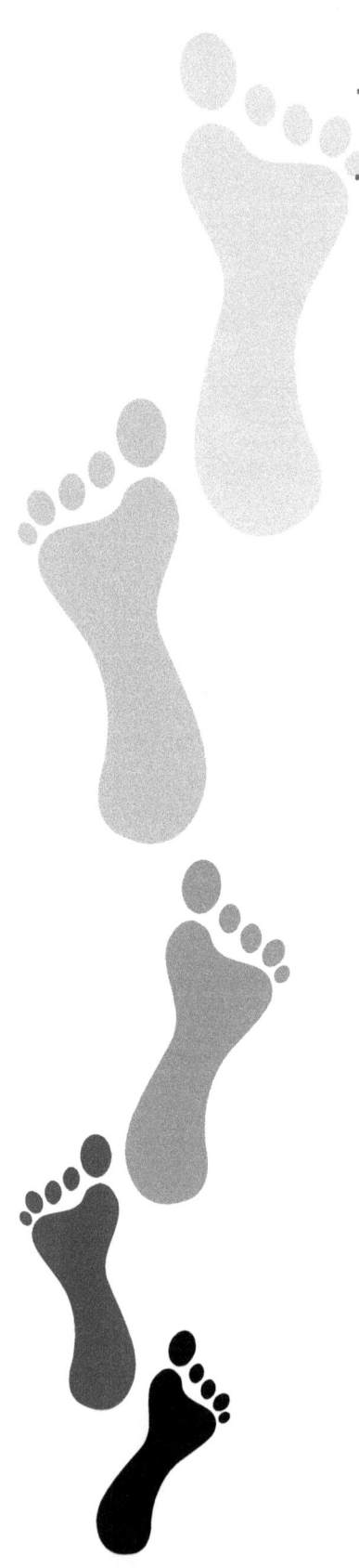

Music

In music, paths were
made by Lena Horne and
Marian Anderson,
From New York's
Broadway to the Lincoln
Memorial steps in
Washington.

Lena Horne

Marian Anderson

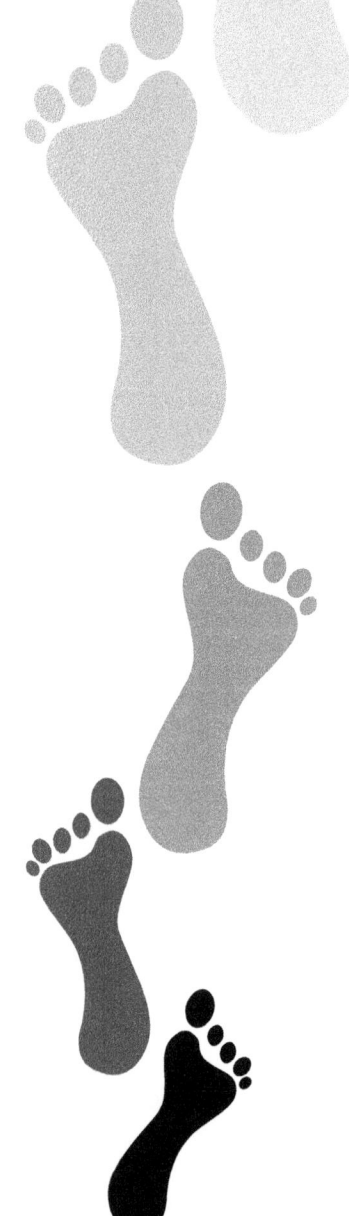

Sports

Baseball/Basketball

First paths in sports, were made in baseball and basketball, by Jackie Robinson and Bill Russell, who are now in Fame Hall.

Jackie Robinson

Bill Russell

Education

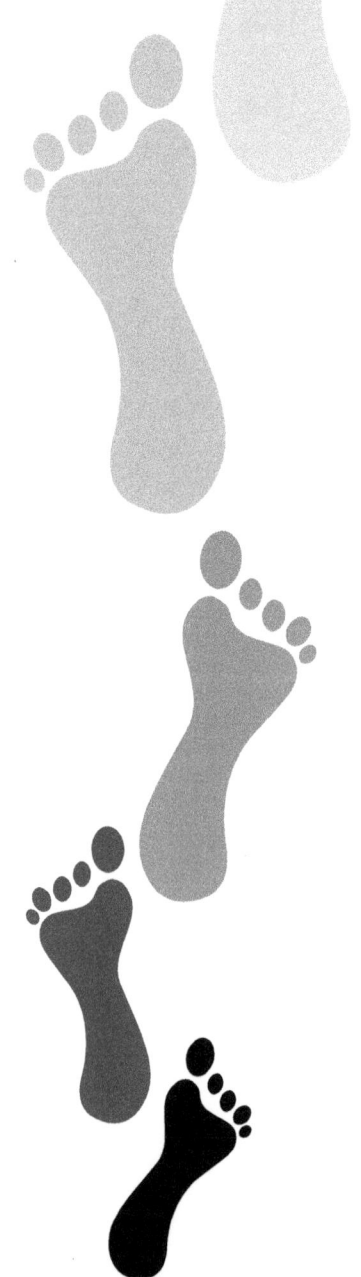

In education,

Booker T. Washington and

Mary McCleod Bethune

opened the first door,

By founding schools to teach

the black and poor.

Booker T. Washington

Mary McCleod Bethune

Poets

Steps were made in poetry by

Langston Hughes and

James Weldon Johnson.

As they wrote about our beautiful

people and God's great creation.

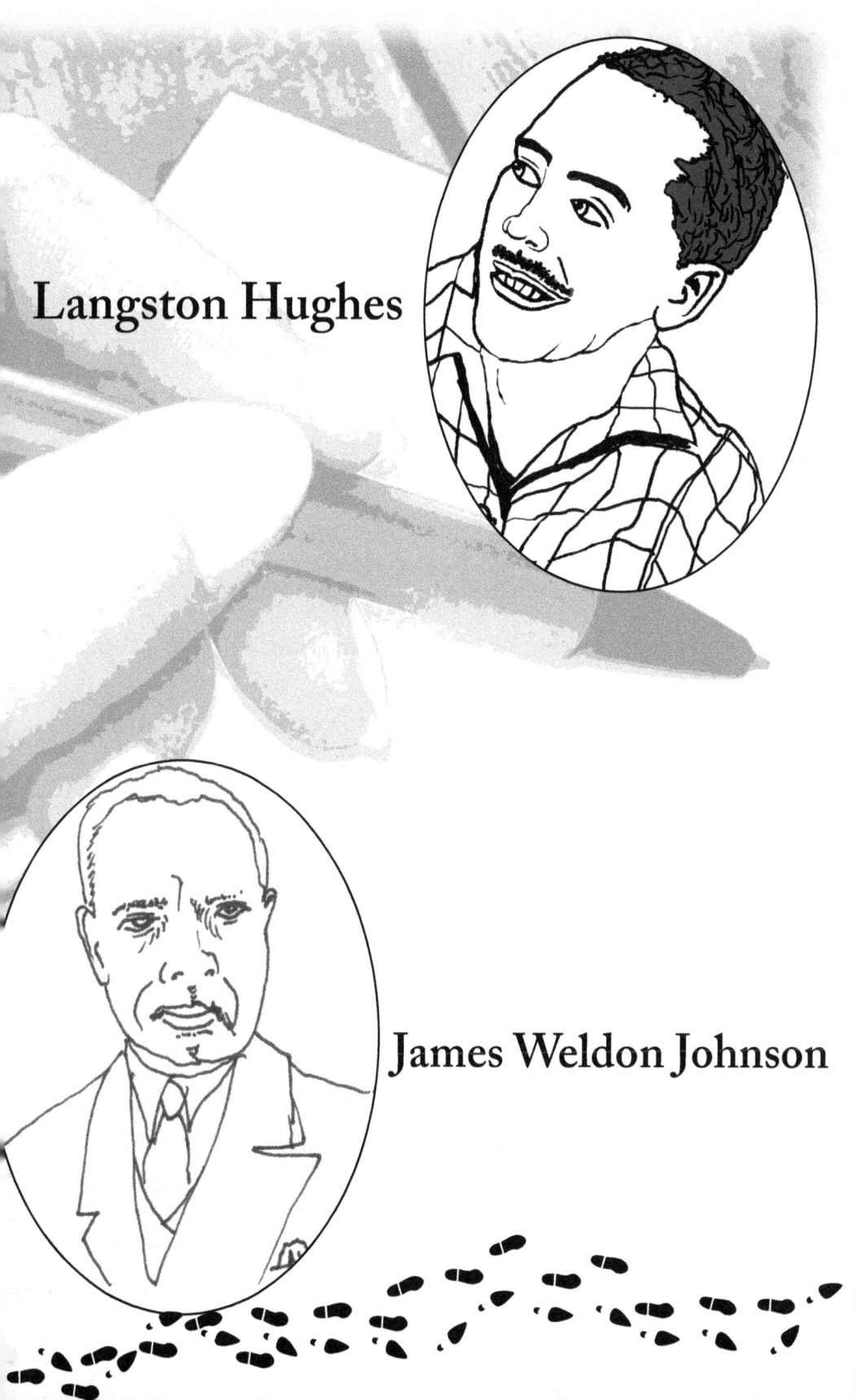

Langston Hughes

James Weldon Johnson

Law & Justice

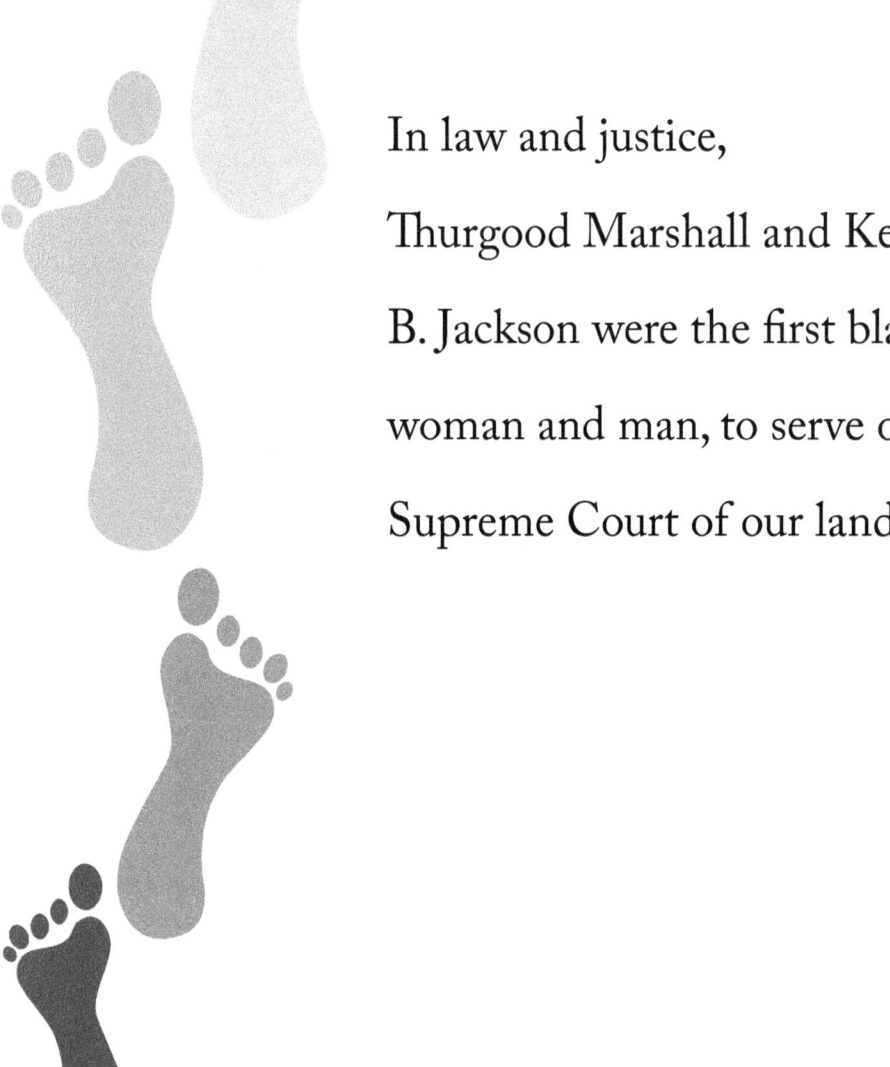

In law and justice,
Thurgood Marshall and Ketanji
B. Jackson were the first black
woman and man, to serve on the
Supreme Court of our land.

Thurgood Marshall

Ketanji B. Jackson

Finance/Business

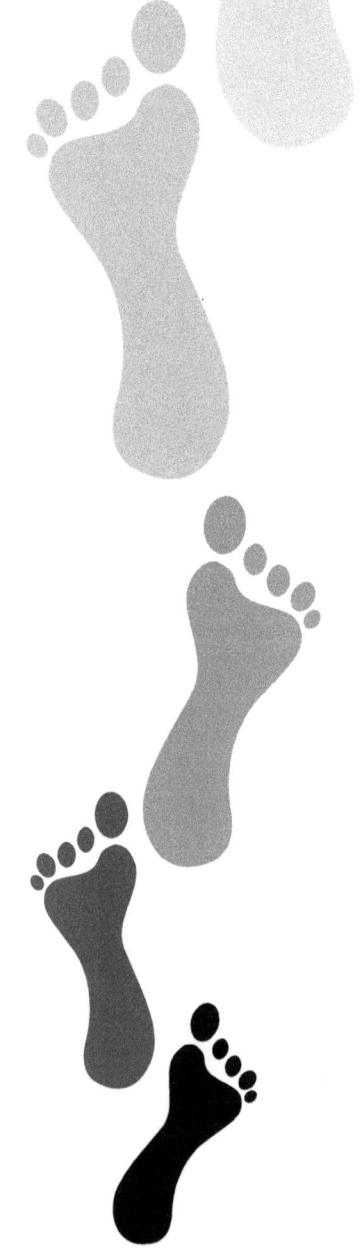

Great financial power,

Madam C.J. Walker, Tyler Perry,

and Oprah Winfrey did show,

As they established businesses

and created products that made

our hair grow.

Madam C.J. Walker

Tyler Perry

Oprah Winfrey

Pilots/Soldiers

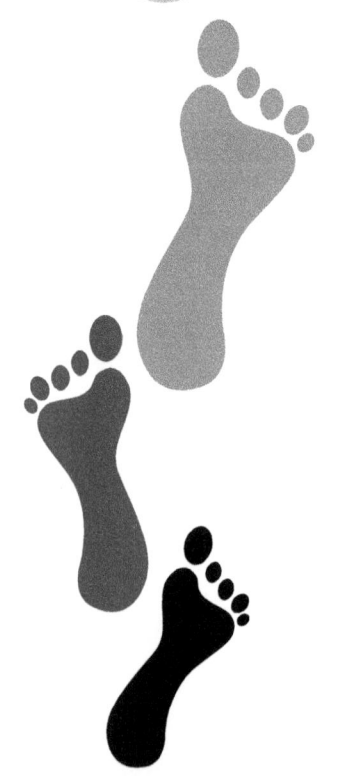

Charles McGee and Colin Powell

made paths on land and in the sky

as they took flight,

And bravely, for our country's

freedom, they did fight.

Charles McGee

Colin Powell

Physicists

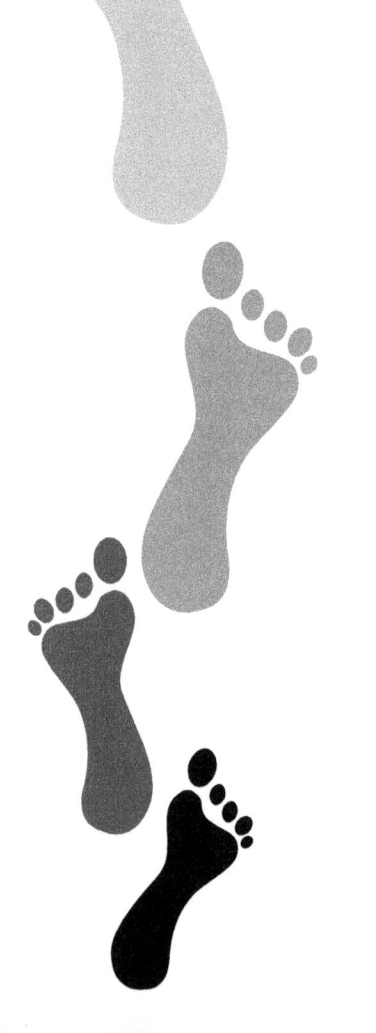

The Three Hidden Figures,

for us made a place, as

Katherine Johnson, Mary Jackson,

and Dorothy Vaughan helped

others travel into space.

Katherine Johnson

Mary Jackson

Dorothy Vaughan

President
Vice
President

Barack Obama and

Kamala Harris opened

the White House Door,

And took seats that Blacks had

not sit in before.

Barack Obama

Kamala Harris

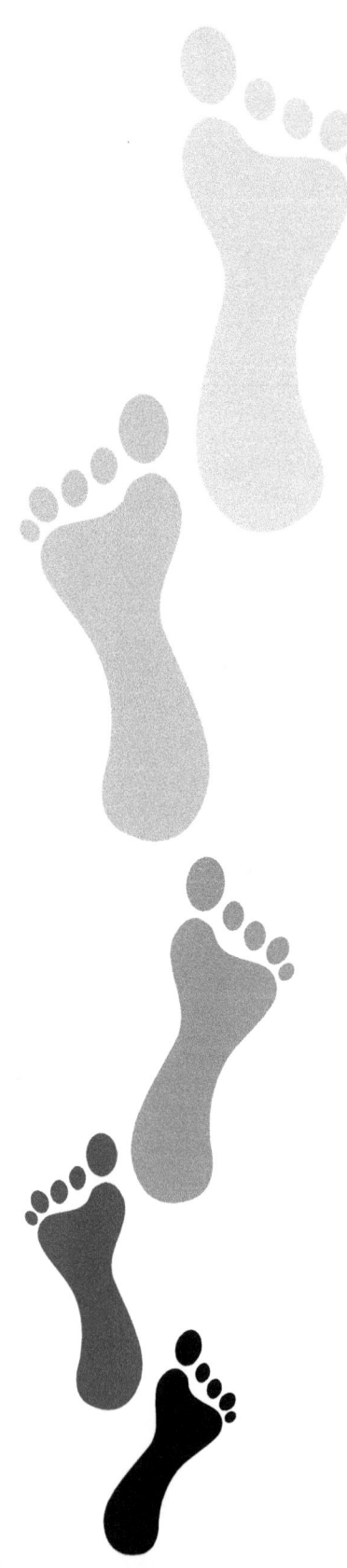

Tennis

In tennis, Serena Williams and

Venus Williams made

their dad very proud,

As they won many championships

before the Wimbledon crowd.

Serena Williams

Venus Williams

In history there are many tracks,

Made by our people we call Blacks.

So choose the one that you would like

to follow,

And you too can become the next

black scholar.

And build another bridge of pride and inspiration,

Which will help others reach their destination.

THE
END

Pages to Color

Pages to Color

Pages to Color

www.ingramcontent.com/pod-product-compliance
Lightning Source LLC
Chambersburg PA
CBHW051244120626
46547CB00014B/1795